follow
in His
footsteps

a holy land pilgrimage journal

Follow In His Footsteps
A Holy Land Pilgrimage Journal

introduction

write about it .. 5

part 1

before you go

change the former way - aptitude 1 .. 8

build on bedrock - aptitude 2 .. 10

know no burden - aptitude 3 .. 12

reconcile with all - aptitude 4 .. 14

be fruitful - aptitude 5 .. 16

always give thanks - aptitude 6 .. 24

more than enough - aptitude 7 .. 26

don't be discouraged - aptitude 8 .. 28

follow in his footsteps - aptitude 9 .. 30

part 2

the holy land

the promised land - the sea of galilee .. 33

the mount of beatitudes - up a mountain .. 36

for a few days - Capernaum .. 39

i've seen the lord - magdala .. 42

full of the spirit - the jordan river .. 45

let justice rain - tel dan .. 48

come and see - nazareth .. 51

closed up tightly - jericho .. 54

part 2 (con't)

the holy land

the strong man - masada & the dead sea .. 57

david's village - bethlehem .. 60

sitting on the mount - jerusalem .. 63

i will bow down - the temple mount .. 66

cross on his back - the via dolorosa .. 69

a place called the skull - holy sepulchre .. 72

part 3

pilgrimage

better than a thousand .. 75

irrevocable .. 76

introduction

write about it

When the men had prepared to go,
Joshua gave orders to those going to write a description of the land.
"Go and travel around the land, write about it, and return to me."
Joshua 18:8 (CEB)

This journal is designed for those traveling to the Holy Land. However, there is work for you to do before you ever pack your bags. This journal is intended to be both read and used before you go and while you are there. When you are in the Holy Land, you will experience sites in ways that may never be fully articulated. Thus, don't think of this as a travel guide. Rather, think of this book as a spiritual guide, prompting you to reflect on both what you want to experience, and also on what you actually experience.

The first section, *Before You Go*, consists of nine aptitudes. These are spiritual prompts for you to reflect on and consider before leaving for the Holy Land. The second section, aptly titled *The Holy Land*, is designed to help you reflect on what you see once in the Holy Land. This is by no means an exhaustive collection of every site you may see. Rather, it is a cause for pause as you journey in the footsteps of Jesus.

The third section, called *Pilgrimage*, is designed to help you examine what this trip meant to you. This section only has two devotionals, but plenty of prompts for you to journal while you are still in the Holy Land, or after you return home.

The land is holy because it is God's gift. While still in Egyptian captivity, God promised Moses and the people that this holy land would be "a good and broad land, a land flowing with milk and honey (Exodus 3:8, NRSV)." It was long awaited, and Joshua was sure to charge his scouts, years later, to write everything they saw in this holy land so that he could apportion the land appropriately.

Our work on this journey is much different from that of Joshua. Nonetheless, use this book as your resource and journal. So, in the words of Joshua "go and travel around the land and write about it."

How do you plan to make this pilgrimage holy?

I plan to ask God to be with us at each of these Holy sites and to reflect Jesus' Light to be an example to others. As I do now give thanks and praise to my Father in Heaven for blessing us with this trip to discover and learn about this land that He chose for His People, I will also give thanks and praise throughout this journey and I will worship in the spirit and truth.

change the former way

Change the former way of life
that was part of the person you once were.
Ephesians 4:22 (CEB)

You may have decided to travel to the Holy Land to have one of those once-in-a-lifetime trips. Because, after all, change is something that you know needs to happen. Paul tells the church in Ephesus to "change the former way of life," and we can relate because we all have things in our lives that deserve a change. Maybe, we think, if we just go somewhere (like the Holy Land), things will change.

You are not alone. People rush to exotic islands to get away. People hop on motorcycles to feel a sense of freedom. We all seek some taste of paradise with a hope that finding that "promised land," things will change.

Escaping, though, is not a sufficient way to face your struggles. In order to change anything, we must actually come face-to-face with our own realities. Even though it can be horribly frightening, the truth is when we face our own issues directly, we become liberated. Father Greg Boyle works with gang members in Los Angeles. He writes "the discovery that awaits us is that paradise is contained in the here and now." Before you go somewhere else, first recognize the paradise contained here.[1]

Paul wrote "change the former way of life."
What things do you need to change?

I need to completed rid sin from
my life. To live righteous in the
eyes of God. When tempted turn
away immediately. Always ready to
testify for Jesus, always willing
to do Gods will.

build on bedrock

Everybody who hears these words of mine and puts them into practice is like a wise builder who built a house on bedrock.

Matthew 7:24 (CEB)

This journal offers some steps to take before you go to the Holy Land to prepare and get your life spiritually and emotionally ready. The first step is to change your former ways, and the best way to go about that is to come face-to-face with your realities, rather than escape them. What follows are several spiritual practices to help you do just that. However, before we can start to build our life with those spiritual tools, we need to lay a solid foundation.

In Matthew and Luke, Jesus teaches us how to build our lives. Wise ones lay their foundations on solid ground. Sinking sand deceives us. We might think it gives us stability, but over time, it will collapse. This parable, then, teaches us mostly about deception. The biggest deceiver in our lives is ourselves. We often convince ourselves that we are in the right. We justify our bad habits. We dismiss others and God and take credit for our own accomplishments.

Our lies, though, are built on sandy ground. The stories we tell ourselves will eventually collapse. Only a life built on bedrock will survive the pending storms. The bedrock, the solid ground we ought to lay our foundations on, is Jesus himself.

How would you describe your foundation?
How can Jesus be your bedrock?

....

....

....

....

....

....

....

....

....

....

....

....

....

....

....

....

know no burden

My yoke is easy to bear, and my burden is light.
Matthew 11:29 (CEB)

Living a Godly life is anything but easy. Paul reminds us that we "all have sinned and fall short of the glory of God (Romans 3:23, NRSV)." Sometimes our sinfulness comes to us more naturally than living a life with God. Trying to do good, while admirable, is also burdensome. Sin can weigh us down, but so can the stress of falling short from trying to do good.

Martin Luther offers some strange advice. He wrote, "sin boldly." The sixteenth-century reformer well understood the biblical concept of sin. Even so, he understood the biblical promise of God's grace even more. He wrote "be a sinner, and sin boldly, but let your trust in Christ be stronger." Luther's hyperbole is wisdom that understands Jesus' words for us to come to him, in our weakness and burden-filled lives. Jesus promises to give us rest. Luther didn't say be the worst sinner, just make sure your love and trust in God is bolder than your boldest sin.

The fact is, when we sin, our flawed lives burden others. We are experts at blaming others and afflicting nonsense. More so, we know others who have burdened us. Our friends, colleagues, and even family members can stress us with all of their own issues. But, know no burden. In other words, rest in Jesus, the one - the only one - who doesn't burden us.

What would things be like if you were less burdened?

I think it's better to consider and take on more burden but only of the fight. Letting go of worldly burdens and living in Christ.

reconcile with all

*All this is from God, who reconciled us to himself through Christ
and gave us the ministry of reconciliation.*

2 Corinthians 5:18 (NIV®)

Traditionally, the church has linked reconciliation with confession. "The Reconciliation of a Penitent" found in the Book of Common Prayer is a rite of confession. While we can confess our sins anywhere, most worship services have specific prayers of confession. However, if worship, or the basic pattern of liturgy found in a Sunday service, is a signpost toward the larger story of God and his love for the world, then a prayer of confession is merely a signpost to live a life of reconciliation.

When an accountant reconciles her ledger with a bank account record, she is making sure the two documents have agreement. Reconciliation, or as Paul says "the ministry of reconciliation," is no different. In reconciliation the two subjects (either God and me, or me and another person) find agreement. This is why the church links confession to reconciliation, because so often when we want to find the good in another, some confession and forgiveness need to take place.

We confess our sin to God, and God forgives. We open to pour out our hearts to another and pray they forgive us. Likewise, even if the other doesn't reconcile with us, we are nonetheless called to forgive them.

What do you need to make right and who do you need to forgive?

....
....
....
....
....
....
....
....
....
....
....
....
....
....
....
....
....

be fruitful

But the fruit of the Spirit is love, joy, peace, patience, kindness,
goodness, faithfulness, gentleness, and self-control.

Galatians 5:22 (CEB)

Confession, forgiveness, fasting, study, fellowship, and prayer are core spiritual disciplines. Yet, what good are any of these if we don't seek to be fruitful? Fruitfulness is a key biblical theme. The promised land, in fact, is "a land of wheat and barley, of vines and fig trees and pomegranates, a land of olive trees and honey (Deuteronomy 8:8, NRSV)." Fruit is one of these images the Bible uses to demonstrate God's abundance in our life.

Hence, aligning our lives to the fruit of the Spirit is validating God's abundance. Love, peace, patience, kindness, goodness, faithfulness, gentleness, and self-control are pathways to an abundant and full life. All of creation, Paul says, waits in "eager expectation," and in this waiting "we ourselves, who have the first fruits of the Spirit, groan inwardly as we wait eagerly (Romans 8:22-23, NIV®)." In other words, even in our own weakness, the Holy Spirit is working.

It is the Holy Spirit that produces the fruit - the love, joy, peace, and so forth. Accepting the Holy Spirit's work in your own life, thus, is the beginning of living a fruitful life.

How can you show more love to others?

....
....
....
....
....
....
....
....
....
....
....
....
....
....
....
....

How can you live more joyfully?

....
....
....
....
....
....
....
....
....
....
....
....
....
....
....
....

What does living a good life mean to you?

What are some of the kindest things you've ever done?

....
....
....
....
....
....
....
....
....
....
....
....
....
....
....
....

Write about the most gentle person you've ever encountered.

....
....
....
....
....
....
....
....
....
....
....
....
....
....
....
....
....

How would you describe your own faithfulness?

....
....
....
....
....
....
....
....
....
....
....
....
....
....
....
....

Where do you need to have more self-control?

....

....

....

....

....

....

....

....

....

....

....

....

....

....

....

....

....

always give thanks

Give thanks to the Lord because he is good,
because his faithful love lasts forever!
Psalm 107:1 (CEB)

Oliver Sacks, British neurologist and one of the greatest scientists of all time, is also one of our greatest teachers in the art of gratitude. Upon learning that he had terminal cancer, he wrote:

> I cannot pretend I am without fear. But my predominant feeling is one of gratitude. I have loved and been loved; I have been given much and I have given something in return; I have read and traveled and thought and written.[2]

We are called to give thanks to the Lord. We are called to live a life of thanksgiving. Yet, can you say what Oliver Sacks has said? Can you say "my predominant feeling is one of gratitude?" Most of us can't. However, most of us ought too.

Living a life of gratitude is not giving thanks for the bad things in life. Rather, it is recognizing that good things actually do outweigh the bad. Thus, there is rarely an opportunity that we can't authentically say "thank you." After all, it only takes a second or two to utter those two words. It is also doesn't take long to look for the experiences in life that manifest gratitude. So watch and then thank.

What do you need to give thanks for?

....
....
....
....
....
....
....
....
....
....
....
....
....
....
....
....
....
....

more than enough

God has the power to provide you
with more than enough of every kind of grace.

2 Corinthians 9:8 (CEB)

Most of us wouldn't mind having a nicer car or fancier house. We live in a consumer-oriented culture, and the lure of bigger and better is real. So when Paul says God has the power to provide you with "more than enough," try not to read into his words thoughts generated from a capitalistic mindset. Instead, think of Paul saying something akin to "be content with what you have."

Contentment is an amazing blessing that most of us can't even begin to comprehend. Moreover, Paul encouraged the church in Corinth to be so content that it shared freely everything it had (read the full chapter). A disposition of contentment, in other words, fosters an attitude of generosity. Even if you aren't aware, contentment and generosity are characteristics found in someone who trusts in God's provision.

Having enough isn't always objectified. We can be content in much more than just having enough things. The challenge, of course, is finding contentment in your relationships, your prayer life, your service, and your attitude. It is God, though, who blesses us, and God has already blessed you abundantly. Be content and assured of this gift of grace.

What would it look like if you were content in a relationship?

....

....

....

....

....

....

....

....

....

....

....

....

....

....

....

....

dont be discouraged

Don't be discouraged!
Don't be afraid! Don't panic! Don't shake in fear.
Deuteronomy 20:3 (CEB)

Meditate, exercise, volunteer, sleep well, eat and drink wisely. These are all pro tips on reducing anxiety and fear. Self-care is critically essential for sure, but still not complete. One of the biggest challenges in lowering our levels of discouragement, fears and times of panic is our own core beliefs or worldview.

Carol Dweck, a psychology professor at Stanford and author of the book *Mindset*, argues we operate with either a fixed mindset or a growth mindset. Getting by on a fixed mindset is relying on your basic traits like talent and intelligence to foster a successful life. Dweck suggests that it is not only lazy, it ends up in disaster. Instead, we need to adopt a growth mindset. We need to continue to develop our basic traits through lifelong learning, trying new things, being resilient, and flexible. Practice does make perfect - or at least better.

A growth mindset proposes that if something goes wrong, discouragement should be only temporary. We can adjust and pick up the pieces and move forward. Christianity has growth practices as well. Read the scripture, pray, serve, and even pilgrimage. The more we practice, the more we can grow in our own faith, less discouraged we will become.

Write about a time you helped someone who was discouraged?

....

....

....

....

....

....

....

....

....

....

....

....

....

....

....

....

follow in his footsteps

You were called to this kind of endurance,
because Christ suffered on your behalf.
He left you an example so that you might follow in his footsteps.

1 Peter 2:21 (CEB)

Soon you will be walking in the footsteps of Jesus the Messiah. When Jesus walked among us, Palestine was divided into three provinces of the Roman Empire – Samaria, Judea, and Galilee. It is a diverse land offering the wilderness of the Judean Desert to the bustling streets of Jerusalem. During your Holy Land visit, you may pass through all three regions. You might sail across the Sea of Galilee and step foot in many of the villages mentioned in the Gospels. You most likely will meditate on the Mount of Beatitudes, visit Jesus' hometown of Nazareth, swim in the Dead Sea, stand atop the Mount of Olives, and walk through the Garden of Gethsemane.

A pilgrimage, however, isn't a mission, a vacation, or an excursion. Our task isn't to visit sites that may or may not be holy, take a picture, and then return home never changed. A pilgrimage is also much more than an expedition. Thankfully, during this visit, there is nothing for us to conquer. There is no peak to climb that sets us apart from others, not an accomplishment to savor. Preferably a pilgrimage, if done with intention, is a journey that collides all of your heart, soul, and might.

Our Jewish brothers and sisters have a journeying phrase. They say "*Shema Yisrael*," which means "Hear, O Israel." The Shema is the foundational summons of the Jewish faith. They say: "The LORD is our God, the LORD alone. You shall love the LORD your God with all your heart, and with all your soul, and with all your might." Jesus repeated these words from Deuteronomy 6:4-5 and added, "this is the greatest and first commandment. And a second is like it: "You shall love your neighbor as yourself (Matthew 22:39, NRSV)."

While pilgrimaging in the holiest of all lands, listen for God's call to pilgrimage, to journey a well-intended collision between the heart, soul, and might. To do this, to enter into such a pilgrimage, you will have to leave a lot behind. Worries and burdens cannot occupy your minds. Internal chatter and distractions must wait for another time. It is now time to settle yourself. To be present. To focus. To listen! You are about to walk in the footsteps of Jesus the Christ. Therefore, listen to the sounds that fill the air. Look with keen eyes. Smell the scents of modern Israel and Palestine. Place your hands on the Western Wall and feel its ragged edges. Taste the authentic meals that Jesus would have tasted. But, most importantly, *Shema Yisrael.* Hear God's call.

How do you plan to be more
focused and present on this pilgrimage?

....
....
....
....
....
....
....
....
....
....
....
....
....
....
....

the promised land

He woke up and rebuked the wind, and said to the sea, "Peace! Be still!"
Mark 4:39 (NRSV)

The land of Canaan, the promised land, was bordered by the small, seven by thirteen-mile, Sea of Galilee. The Gospel of Luke rightly calls this freshwater body a lake. The Sea of Galilee, called Lake Gennesaret in Luke's gospel, is at the center of Jesus' public ministry. The Jordan flows from its north and south. Bethsaida, where many of his disciples are from, is directly north of the Sea. Tiberias, Magdala, and Capernaum surround its shores.

The Sea of Galilee is surrounded (except the south) by steep hills, and thus harsh winds are known to whip up sporadically. One afternoon Jesus was resting on a boat as the disciples fished the gentle sea. Perhaps it was one of these sporadic winds, a "huge storm", says Matthew, that frightened everyone, but Jesus (Matthew 8:24, CEB).

The Psalmist writes "You rule over the surging sea: When its waves rise up, it's you who makes them still (Psalm 89:9, CEB)." Jesus knew these words, but he was not pleased that his disciples seemed not to believe them. The same goes for us. During the storms of our lives, we often forget how much power God has to make things calm.

Describe a time you didn't rely on God
to calm a storm in your life.

What are your reflections on the
Sea of Galilee?

....

....

....

....

....

....

....

....

....

....

....

....

....

....

....

up a mountain

Now when Jesus saw the crowds, he went up a mountain.

Matthew 5:1 (CEB)

The Gospel of Matthew tells us that Jesus preached from the mountain. Saint Augustine, a critically important theologian from the turn of the fifth century, was the first to call these words from Jesus "The Sermon on the Mount." The sermon begins with the "Beatitudes" which are a series of eight blessings. The word beatitude is derived from the Latin word that means blessing.

After the Beatitudes (or blessings from Jesus), Jesus says "you are the light of world...let your light shine (Matthew 5:14,16)." He continues to the tough subjects of murder, adultery, divorce, and revenge. Then Jesus says "love your enemies and pray for those who persecute you (5:44)." After he addresses service to the poor, he prays what we know as the Lord's Prayer. He continues to discuss fasting, idolatry, worry, judging others, and toward the sermon's conclusion he says "ask and it will be given to you; seek and you will find; knock and the door will be opened to you (Matthew 7:7, NRSV)."

Jesus' sermon is both uplifting and challenging. Living a faithful life, though, isn't about getting everything right. Instead, faithfulness is about asking, seeking, and knocking, and discovering the ways God answers.

What are some things you ought to
seek, ask, and knock on God's door for?

....

....

....

....

....

....

....

....

....

....

....

....

....

....

....

....

What are your reflections on the
Mount of Beatitudes?

....
....
....
....
....
....
....
....
....
....
....
....
....
....
....
....
....

for a few days

After this, Jesus and his mother, his brothers, and his disciples
went down to Capernaum and stayed there for a few days.

John 2:12 (CEB)

Capernaum is central to Jesus' ministry. Jesus healed a centurion's servant in Capernaum. In Mark's gospel, Jesus exercises the first demon he encounters in Capernaum. He heals and forgives there, and this is where Jesus entered that famous boat journey across the Sea of Galilee when the winds whipped up and frightened the disciples.

Both Matthew (9:1) and Mark (2:1) call Capernaum Jesus' home. It is also the home of Levi, the tax collector. Jesus said to Levi "follow me, and Levi got up, left everything behind, and followed him (Luke 5:27-28, CEB)." After this, Levi threw Jesus a massive party at his Capernaum home.

While in Capernaum, imagine Jesus saying to you "follow me." Would you respond the way Levi did? Dietrich Bonhoeffer, the German Lutheran pastor who was imprisoned and executed by Hitler, wrote: "we are not called to contemplate the disciple [i.e. Levi], but only him who calls…there is no road to faith or discipleship, no other road - only obedience to the call of Jesus."[3]

Where is God calling and leading you?

....
....
....
....
....
....
....
....
....
....
....
....
....
....
....
....
....

What are your reflections on
Capernaum?

....
....
....
....
....
....
....
....
....
....
....
....
....
....

ive seen the lord

Mary Magdalene left and announced to the disciples,
"I've seen the Lord."
Then she told them what he said to her.

John 20:18 (CEB)

We don't know much about Magdala, or as most Greek manuscripts of Matthew 15:39 say "Magadan." We do know, however, that all four gospels mention Mary Magdalene or Mary of Magdala. Mary was a common name. Mary Magdalene wasn't Jesus' mother, Martha's sister (John 11), or Clopas' wife (John 19:25). Mary also isn't the mother of James (Matthew 27:55) or John Mark (Acts 12:12). So, who was she?

Mary Magdalene most definitely was not a prostitute, as some Jesus films portray her. Pope Gregory I managed to get that rumor started in the seventh century. Mary Magdalene was, in fact, in Jesus' inner circle. Many scholars believe she was his "beloved disciple" as referenced in the gospel of John (see 21:20 for example). There is no doubt that Mary Magdalene was a benefactor of Jesus' ministry (Matthew 27:55-56).

Mary Magdalene's most notable deed is also her least known. If to preach the gospel is to proclaim Christ's resurrection, then she was our very first preacher. It was Mary Magdalene who first said "I've seen the Lord."

What would it take for you to be called the "beloved disciple?"

....
....
....
....
....
....
....
....
....
....
....
....
....
....
....
....
....

What are your reflections on
Magdala?

....

....

....

....

....

....

....

....

....

....

....

....

....

....

....

full of the spirit

Jesus returned from the Jordan River full of the Holy Spirit.

Luke 4:1 (CEB)

You will not find the River Jordan on anyone's rankings of most beautiful bodies of water. The pictures you take will not be impressive. The water is brown and narrow. The area may be crowded. However, beauty isn't always a matter of appearance. Instead, what makes the Jordan particularly impressive is its history. Joshua, Elisha, Elijah, Naaman, and John the Baptist had powerful spiritual encounters in the Jordan, as did Jesus. The Protestant reformer Martin Luther wrote this hymn, set in composition by Bach:

> *To Jordan when our Lord had gone,*
> *His Father's pleasure willing,*
> *He took His baptism of St John,*
> *His work and task fulfilling.*[4]

The River Jordan is the place where Jesus went to be baptized by John. John resisted, of course, but as soon as Jesus was baptized, the heavens opened up. You, like Jesus, may walk into the River Jordan, to the "Father's pleasure willing." It is possible, in fact, to be baptized in the Jordan. If not, remember your baptismal vows in the very place Jesus was immersed by John, as you allow these holy waters to renew your soul.

What things most renew your soul?

*What are your reflections on
the River Jordan?*

let justice rain

Hate evil, love good,
and establish justice at the city gate.
Perhaps the Lord God of heavenly forces
will be gracious to what is left of Joseph.

Amos 5:15 (CEB)

Cities of antiquity had gates. Tel Dan is no exception. A city's gate was its center of commerce and culture. The prophet Amos declares "establish justice at the city gate." Admittedly, Amos isn't too confident. He says "perhaps" God may be gracious. The conditions people found themselves in at the city's gate in Tel Dan and across Israel was bleak. The northern kingdom (Israel), in fact, ended by the Assyrian invasion during Amos' lifetime.

Things don't always go our way. Israel knew this. What we establish often gets unraveled and torn apart. Sometimes we fail to hate evil and sometimes we aren't any good at loving what is good. Sometimes we flounder at God's command to establish justice in the center of our communities. Like Israel, sometimes we simply get defeated. Amos' half-hearted promise that "perhaps" God would be gracious is nonetheless a promise. Despite who Israel was, God would be gracious. Despite who we are, and what we have done and left undone, God remains gracious.

Describe a time when God's has been gracious,
even though you feel you weren't deserving.

....
....
....
....
....
....
....
....
....
....
....
....
....
....
....
....
....
....

What are your reflections on
Tel Dan?

....
....
....
....
....
....
....
....
....
....
....
....
....
....
....
....
....
....

come and see

Nathanael responded,
"Can anything from Nazareth be good?"
Philip said, "Come and see."

John 1:46 (CEB)

Before Jesus started acting like the Messiah by preaching of God's coming kingdom, healing the sick, cleansing the unclean, demonstrating miracles and signs, and suffering to the point of death and rising on the third day, he lived in the village of Nazareth.

In Matthew's gospel, we sense that the people who knew or encountered Jesus while in Nazareth were surprised. Alternatively, even if they didn't know him, they were surprised that the Messiah grew up in Nazareth. After all, he was merely "the carpenter's son (Matthew 13:5, CEB)." It is said that "familiarity breeds contempt." Is this the case here? Even Nathanael asked in John's gospel: "Can anything from Nazareth be good?"

Philip, who was with Nathanael said, "come and see." The fact is, good can be found anywhere, not because the Messiah once lived there, but because he is present there now. The beauty of our faith is that we affirm Jesus the Christ is present with us always, in and through all circumstances. "Come and see" Jesus the Emmanuel, "God with us (Matthew 1:23)."

Philip said, "come and see."
Who in your life has invited you to "come and see?"

*What are your reflections on
Nazareth?*

....
....
....
....
....
....
....
....
....
....
....
....
....
....
....

closed up tightly

Now Jericho was closed up tightly.

Joshua 6:1 (CEB)

Perhaps because of its fertility amid the exhausting desert, Jericho is claimed to be one of the oldest cities on earth. It plays a critical role in the book of Joshua as the Israelites destroyed almost everything within. This violent command is hard to grasp, and even so the New Testament book claims it was "by faith the walls of Jericho fell (11:30, NRSV)."

Joshua chapter six is full of inconsistencies. More so, there is absolutely no reliable archeological evidence of any collapsed walls. Nonetheless, the story remains powerful for many reasons. Most obvious, is that the Israelites focused on exhibiting the power of God. Sometimes we go too far and attribute things to God's power that God might not deserve. God may not appreciate being viewed as the Lord of holy wars.

The faith, the book of Hebrews mentions, may also be that of Rahab. Rahab and her family is spared this destruction. As an innkeeper, Rahab showed hospitality to God's people. James' letter in the New Testament claims Rahab was a prostitute, demonstrating that God finds worth in all people despite their past. Most interestingly she is found in the genealogy of Jesus in Matthew's gospel as the mother of Boaz.

When have you encountered hospitality
from someone who you wouldn't expect it?

....

....

....

....

....

....

....

....

....

....

....

....

....

....

....

....

....

What are your reflections on
Jericho?

....
....
....
....
....
....
....
....
....
....
....
....
....
....
....
....

the strong man

But no one can enter a strong man's house and plunder his property
without first tying up the strong man;
then indeed the house can be plundered.

Mark 3:27 (NRSV)

Herod the Great, the "king of the Jews," built the impressive mountaintop fortress, Masada, with breath-taking views of the Dead Sea. Masada isn't mentioned in the Bible, and the Dead Sea is only mentioned briefly. However, both Masada and the Dead Sea are significant to the Jewish and Christian faiths.

The Herodian family governed Palestine under the authority of the Roman Empire for quite some time, and Masada is representative of the dominance of the empire Jesus called the "strong man" in Mark's gospel. New Testament scholar John Dominic Crossan writes "the Bible was filled with pleas for mercy, cries for clemency, and prayers for forgiveness...an appeal for divine deliverance from imperial oppression."[5]

It is natural to be inspired by the extraordinary Masada fortress. However, pilgrims to the Holy Land should consider the notable consequences and fallout determined by an imperial rule. Oppression from domination systems still affects our world today. Yet, our God is a God of justice and Jesus was determined to reveal God's alternative and remarkable kingdom.

In what ways can you reveal God's alternative kingdom?

....
....
....
....
....
....
....
....
....
....
....
....
....
....
....
....

What are your reflections on
Masada and the Dead Sea?

....
....
....
....
....
....
....
....
....
....
....
....
....
....
....

davids village

Didn't the scripture say
that the Christ comes from David's family
and from Bethlehem, David's village?

John 7:42 (CEB)

There may not be a more famous place than the little town of Bethlehem. Perhaps when both David and Jesus were born in Bethlehem, it was reserved and picturesque. Not so much today. The streets are no longer whimsical, but rather noisy and crowded. The perfect place, actually, for the savior of the world to be born.

Saint Jerome, the great Catholic theologian, and translator of the Bible, retired in Bethlehem in the fifth century. Although the gospels make no mention of any cave, reportedly Jerome lived in the very cave Jesus was born. Jerome is credited with establishing a great monastic community in Bethlehem that lead to Constantine's building of the Church of the Nativity.

The Church of the Nativity is embellished with mosaics, icons, silver, and gold. It is not as adorned as major cathedrals, but Jerome still asked how the church justifies the embellishment of our sanctuaries considering the humble beginnings of Jesus who remained poor his entire life. No matter if we are on the streets of poverty or in the chapel adorned, let us always sing "O holy child of Bethlehem descend to us, we pray."

In what ways have you paid more attention to how your faith appears to others, rather than how your faith really is?

....
....
....
....
....
....
....
....
....
....
....
....
....
....
....
....
....

What are your reflections on
Bethlehem?

....
....
....
....
....
....
....
....
....
....
....
....
....
....
....
....
....

sitting on the mount

Jesus was sitting on the Mount of Olives across from the temple.

Mark 13:3 (CEB)

Jerusalem is the world's most contested city. It seems everyone has a claim on this extraordinary city. The prophet Zechariah teaches that Jerusalem would be far from peaceful. He preached "the city will be captured, the houses will be plundered, and the women will be raped (14:2, CEB)." Regardless, there is something enchanted about Jerusalem. The historian Simon Sebag Montesfiore captures its spellbinding appeal this way:

> This is a place of such delicacy that it is described in Jewish sacred literature in the feminine - always a sensual, living woman, always a beauty, but sometimes a shameless harlot, sometimes a wounded princess whose lovers have forsaken her. Jerusalem is the house of the one God, the capital of two peoples, the temple of three religions and she is the only city to exist twice - in heaven and on earth: the peerless grace of the terrestrial is as nothing to the glories of the celestial. [6]

Zechariah says God one day "will stand upon the Mount of Olives, to the east of Jerusalem (14:4, CEB)." Jesus did just that. As you look beyond the Mount of Olives and see the terrestrial and celestial city of Jerusalem, pray Psalm 122:6:

> *Pray that Jerusalem has peace:*
> *Let those who love you have rest.* (CEB)

Write a prayer for peace in the Holy Land.

What are your reflections on
Jerusalem?

....

....

....

....

....

....

....

....

....

....

....

....

....

....

....

i will bow down

I will enter your house
because of your abundant, faithful love;
I will bow down at your holy temple,
honoring you.

Psalm 5:7 (CEB)

The Temple Mount is the most sacred site in the Jewish faith. The Western Wall is known as the Wailing Wall referring to the mourning of the Temple's destruction. The Mount itself isn't in Jewish hands. Al-Haram al-Sharif, and the Dome of the Rock is the third most holy site in Islam, marking the cite that Muslims believe Muhammad ascended to heaven.

At the Temple's completion, Solomon told God: "I have built you an exalted house, a place for you to dwell in forever. (1 Kings 8:13, NRSV)." The Temple wasn't so exalted in Jesus' mind. In the Synoptic Gospels (Matthew, Mark, and Luke) Jesus encounters controversy in the Temple. In John's gospel, Jesus says: "Destroy this temple and in three days I'll raise it up (John 2:19, CEB)." Of course, Jesus was speaking symbolically and prophetically of the Jerusalem Temple's imminent destruction and his own death.

For Solomon, the Temple represented God's earthly presence. For us, it is at "the name of Jesus every knee should bow (Philippians 2:10, NIV*)."

What places do you go to feel God's presence?
Where have you most experienced God's presence?

....
....
....
....
....
....
....
....
....
....
....
....
....
....
....
....
....
....
....
....

*What are your reflections on
the Temple Mount?*

....
....
....
....
....
....
....
....
....
....
....
....
....
....
....

cross on his back

They compelled a passer-by, who was coming in from the country,
to carry his cross; it was Simon of Cyrene,
the father of Alexander and Rufus.

Mark 15:21 (NRSV)

Over time faithful people have tried to weave the details of Jesus walk to the cross. The Via Dolorosa, or the Way of Sorrows, is a tapestry of biblical and non-biblical histories. Most people identify fourteen stations of the cross, eight having scriptural references.

Although in John's gospel Jesus carries his own cross, the Synoptic gospels say they "forced" Simon from Cyrene to carry Jesus' cross. Some bibles translate it as "seized" him, others say "grabbed" him. The best translation from the Greek word *aggareuō* is "compelled" as the NRSV writes.

There is a lot of irony in Mark's gospel. The disciples are nowhere around, yet Simon just happened to be passing by. In Mark's first chapter it was Jesus who "passed" along the coast and compelled another Simon to follow him. Later in Mark 8, Jesus says: "If any want to become my followers, let them deny themselves and take up their cross and follow me (8:34, NRSV)."

The Way of the Cross is following in the painful and sorrowful, but liberating and freeing, footsteps of Jesus.

In what ways do you relate to Simon from Cyrene?

....
....
....
....
....
....
....
....
....
....
....
....
....
....
....
....

What are your reflections on
the Via Dolorosa?

the holy land - holy sepulchre

a place called the skull

Carrying his cross by himself,
he went out to a place called Skull Place.

John 19:17 (CEB)

Golgotha is an Aramaic word that means skull. We are more familiar with the word derived from the Latin, *calva*, or calvary. Emperor Constantine was certain that Jesus was crucified beneath Hadrian's Temple. Saint Helena (Constantine's mother) sought to find the exact tomb. In her quest, she found three wooden crosses and a placard that read "Jesus of Nazareth, King of the Jews."

Whether Helena's discovery was real or not, her work is forever engraved into the life of Jerusalem, building the Church of the Holy Sepulchre at this now traditional site of Calvary, or Golgotha. Sepulchre derives from the Latin *seperlire* meaning to bury or burial place. Regardless if Helena's story is accurate, the Church of the Holy Sepulchre is the primary Christian pilgrimage destination. It is the one place every follower of Christ ought to visit. The crucifixion of Jesus is paramount to our understanding of Christianity itself.

Orthodox Christians, however, don't call this the Church of the Holy Sepulchre. Instead, they call it the Church of the Anastasis, from the Greek word resurrection. After all, the death of Jesus is only properly understood by his resurrection.

What does the resurrection of Jesus mean to you?

*What are your reflections on
the Church of the Holy Sepulchre?*

....
....
....
....
....
....
....
....
....
....
....
....
....
....
....
....
....

pilgrimage

better than a thousand

For a day in your courts is better than a thousand elsewhere.

Psalm 84:10 (NRSV)

Even though your holy land trip eventually ends, your pilgrimage continues. The sounds, sights, and smells of Palestine and Israel will travel with you forever. You are now linked to the millions of Jewish, Christian, and Muslim pilgrims who have journeyed to the Holy Land for thousands of years. The psalmist, like you, yearned to travel to these holy places with the hopes of experiencing and perhaps even meeting God in God's dwelling place. Consider Psalm 84:1: "How lovely is your dwelling place, Lord Almighty! (NIV*)."

"Lovely" in Hebrew is *yĕdiyd*, a sensual and passionate love and expresses an excessive or fierce affirmation. "Lovely" is a bit weak and surely doesn't give justice to the pilgrim's experience. The Psalm concludes dramatically: "For a day in your courts is better than a thousand elsewhere (84:10, NRSV)." Likewise, may your days in the Holy Land be better than a thousand elsewhere. Like the psalmist you may find that the words you speak to this experience are quite insufficient. This is the mystery of the Holy Land. This is why, when you return home, you will resort to saying to others, "you will just have to go and see for yourself."

pilgrimage

irrevocable

For the gifts and the calling of God are irrevocable.
Romans 11:29 (NRSV)

In the book of Genesis, Jacob was a dreamer. In one of his dreams, he sees a ladder from earth to heaven with angels of God "ascending and descending on it (Genesis 28:12, NRSV)." In many ways, the ladder represents Jacob's constant journey. Rabbi Harold Kushner writes:

> If the ladder that bridges heaven and earth represents the distance between Jacob as he is and Jacob as he would like to be, then his life story is the account...to become a more complete person not through disguise and misrepresentation but through sacrifice and growth.[7]

A pilgrimage is an experience that millions endeavor in a search for God. It is also a journey to find your more complete self. Hence, pilgrimages are key to vocation, for in these searches you may find God's "irrevocable" call. If you have journeyed intending to listen and discover your own aptitudes and the holiness of this land, then you will have heard and seen various sacred callings, glimpses of God's will for your life. Therefore, use the journal pages that follow for you to think theologically about your vocation, and anything else you want to reflect on.

Bethlehem
Naomi & Ruth: Ruth 1
Samuel anoints David: 1 Samuel 16
The birth of Jesus: Luke 2

Capernaum
Jesus heals woman: Mark 5:21-35
Jesus heals servant: Matthew 8: 5-13
Jesus calls Matthew: Mark 2: 13-17

Garden Tomb
The resurrection: John 19:38-20:10

Gethsemane
Jesus' arrest: Mark 14:32-52

Hezekiah's Tunnel
Hezekiah: 2 Chronicles 32:20-33

Jericho
Battle: Joshua 6:1-27
Good Samaritan: Luke 10:25-37
Jesus & Zacchaeus: Luke 19:1-10

Jerusalem
Peace for the city: Psalm 122
Jesus weeps: Luke 19:41-44
Via Dolorosa: Mark 15
Holy Sepulchre: Matthew 27:32-61

Jordan River
Crossing the Jordan: Joshua 2-3
Elijah & Elisha 2 Kings 2:1-23
Jesus' baptism: Matthew 3:13 17

Magdala
Mary's home: Luke 8:1-2
The tomb: Matthew 27:57-66

Mount of Beatitudes
Jesus' sermon: Matthew 5-7

Mount of Olives
David's escape: 2 Samuel 15:13-31
Prophet's vision: Zechariah 14:3-4
Jesus' entry: Matthew 21:1-10
Jesus' ascension: Acts 1:1-12

Nazareth
The annunciation: Luke 1:26-38
Jesus' rejection: Luke 4:16-30

The Pool of Bethesda
Sabbath healing: Matthew 5:1-18

The Pool of Siloam
Blind man healed: John 9:1-41

The Sea of Galilee
Jesus still the storm: Mark 4:35-42
Miraculous catch: Luke 5:1-11
Jesus feeds 5,000: Mark 6:30-44
Jesus walks on water: Mark 6:45-52

Temple Mount
Binding of Isaac: Genesis 22:1-18
The first temple: 2 Chronicles 6:1-11
Rebuilding the temple: Ezra 6:1-15
Cleansing: Mark 11:15-19

works cited

1. Boyle, Greg. *Barking to the Choir: The Power of Radical Kinship*. New York: Simon & Schuster, 2017.

2. Sacks, Oliver. *Gratitude*. First edition. New York: Toronto: Alfred A. Knopf; Alfred A. Knopf of Canada, 2015.

3. Bonhoeffer, Dietrich. *The Cost of Discipleship*. 1st Touchstone ed. New York: Touchstone, 1995.

4. Luther, Martin. "To Jordan came our Lord, the Christ." Hymn 401. *Evangelical Lutheran Hymn-book*. St. Louis: Concordia, 1990.

5. Crossan, John Dominic. *God and Empire : Jesus against Rome, Then and Now*. 1st ed. San Francisco: HarperSanFrancisco, 2007.

6. Sebag Montefiore, Simon. *Jerusalem : The Biography*. London: Weidenfeld & Nicolson, 2011.

7. Kushner, Harold S. *Living a Life That Matters: Resolving the Conflict between Conscience and Success*. 1st ed. New York: A.A. Knopf, 2001.

acknowledgments

This devotional journal has been an exhausting, yet fulfilling project. I need and want to thank the many friends, students, and family who supported this venture. I am blessed by Andrew Burnett, Ben Rogers, Cailee Franklin, and Cameron Burnette for their editing and design skills. I am also thankful for the support of the Lilly Endowment, the Charlotte Presbytery, and the Casey-Peeler Fund for allowing me to take students from the University of North Carolina at Charlotte to the Holy Land. I am thankful for the campus ministry I serve, Niner United, the Episcopal, Lutheran (ELCA), Presbyterian (USA), and United Methodist campus ministry at UNC Charlotte. I am very thankful for the support of Niner United's Board of Directors, the student leaders who serve this ministry, and for Trey O'Quinn who serves as the board chairperson. Finally, I am most grateful for the support of my wife Bridgett, and our kids Alex, Caleb, and Maggie.

56131041R00061

Made in the USA
Middletown, DE
19 July 2019